LOOKING BACK

MESOPOTAMIA
AND THE
FERTILE CRESCENT
10,000 TO 539 B.C.

LOOKING BACK

MESOPOTAMIA
AND THE
FERTILE CRESCENT
10,000 TO 539 B.C.

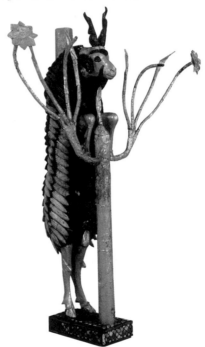

JOHN MALAM

RSVP

RAINTREE
STECK-VAUGHN
PUBLISHERS
A Steck-Vaughn Company

Austin, Texas

Editor: Nicola Barber, Pam Wells
Designer: Neil Sayer
Picture research: Victoria Brooker
Maps: Nick Hawken
Production: Jenny Mulvanny

Consultant: Dr. Alasdair Livingstone, Reader in Assyriology, Department of Ancient History and Archaeology, The University of Birmingham

Library of Congress Cataloging-in-Publication Data

Malam, John.
    Mesopotamia and the fertile crescent, 10,000 to 539 B.C. / John Malam
        p.   cm. — (Looking back)
    Includes bibliographical references (p.   ) and index.
    Summary: Describes ancient Mesopotamia, now located in present-day Iraq, and traces its history, technological innovations, people, and culture from 10,000 to 539 B.C.
    ISBN 0-8172-5434-X
    1. Iraq — Civilization— To 634 — Juvenile literature.   2. Middle East — Civilization — To 622 — Juvenile literature. [1. Iraq — Civilization — To 634 2. Middle East — Civilization — To 622] I. Title.
II. Series.
DS69.5.M27   1999
935 — DC21   98-29665
                                          CIP   AC

Printed in Spain
Bound in the United States
1 2 3 4 5 6 7 8 9 0 LB 02 01 00 99 98

Title page: A golden ram, c. 2600 B.C., from the Great Death Pit at Ur. It is one of a pair which may have been used as furniture supports.

Acknowledgments

cover (background image) British Museum/Bridgeman Art Library (main image)AKG **title page** British Museum **page 6** Ancient Art and Architecture **page 9** Philip Wayre/NHPA **page 12** Daniel O'Leary/Panos Pictures **page 13** David Heath/Life File **page 14** Trip/H Rogers **page 16** Louvre, Paris/Bridgeman Art Library **page 17** British Museum/Bridgeman Art Library **page 19** Louvre, Paris/Bridgeman Art Library **page 20** Ancient Art and Architecture **page 21** Louvre, Paris/Bridgeman Art Library **page 23** British Museum **page 24** British Museum/ Bridgeman Art Library **page 25** Kunsthistorisches Museum, Vienna/Bridgeman Art Library **page 27** Baghdad Museum **page 29** Louvre, Paris/Lauros-Giraudon/Bridgeman Art Library **page 30** British Museum **page 31** AKG Photo **page 32** Ancient Art and Architecture **page 33** British Museum/ Bridgeman Art Library **page 34** Werner Forman **page 35** British Museum **page 36** AKG **page 37** British Museum **page 38** Werner Forman **page 40** British Museum/Bridgeman Art Library **page 41** Louvre, Paris/Lauros-Giraudon/Bridgeman Art Library **page 42** Christine Osborne Pictures **page 43** Private Collection/Bridgeman Art Library **page 44** (top) British Museum/Bridgeman Art Library (bottom) Louvre, Paris/Bridgeman Art Library **page 45** (top) British Museum (bottom) British Museum/Bridgeman Art Library **page 46** Louvre, Paris/Bridgeman Art Library **page 47** British Museum/Bridgeman Art Library **page 48** British Museum/Bridgeman Art Library **page 49** British Museum **page 51** Werner Forman **page 52** Iraq Museum, Baghdad/Bridgeman Art Library **page 53** British Museum **page 54** British Museum/ Bridgeman Art Library **page 55** British Museum **page 56** Ancient Art and Architecture **page 57** British Museum/Bridgeman Art Library **page 58** Trip/B Vikander **page 59** S Kay/Life File

CONTENTS

INTRODUCTION

This book is about an ancient region of the Middle East. The name we use for the area is "Mesopotamia." The book covers about 9,500 years of history, from 10,000 B.C. to 539 B.C.

It was the Ancient Greeks who first called the region Mesopotamia. This was their name for the strip of land that lay between the Euphrates and Tigris rivers, in what is now the modern country of Iraq. Today, however, when historians and archaeologists talk about Mesopotamia they are actually referring to a much wider area covering the whole of Iraq, together with southeastern Turkey and eastern Syria. In ancient times this huge area was home to many different civilizations.

A TALE OF TWO RIVERS

Much of Mesopotamia today is a wide, flat floodplain that lies between the region's two great rivers—the Euphrates, and its faster-flowing neighbor, the Tigris. As they flow southeast through Iraq, the Tigris and the Euphrates rivers join together to form a single river, the Shatt al-Arab, that empties into the Persian Gulf.

Today, the ruins of the city of Ur lie in the middle of an arid floodplain. In ancient times, Ur stood on the banks of the Euphrates River.

The Tigris and Euphrates flood twice each year. The main flood is in April and May when the rivers swell with water from melting winter snow in the northern highlands, and with spring rains. When the rivers crest and flood, vast quantities of sediment are washed

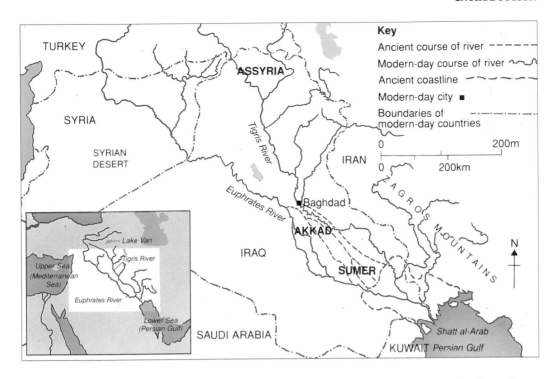

Key
Ancient course of river – – – – –
Modern-day course of river ∿∿
Ancient coastline – – – –
Modern-day city ■
Boundaries of
modern-day countries – · – · –

TURKEY

SYRIA

SYRIAN
DESERT

ASSYRIA

Tigris River

IRAN

Euphrates River

Baghdad

AKKAD

IRAQ

SUMER

ZAGROS MOUNTAINS

N

0   200m
0   200km

Lake Van

Tigris River

Upper Sea
(Mediterranean
Sea)

Euphrates River

Lower Sea
(Persian Gulf)

SAUDI ARABIA

KUWAIT

Shatt al-Arab
Persian Gulf

This map shows both the ancient and present-day courses of the Euphrates and Tigris rivers.

downstream. The sediment is dumped at the head of the Persian Gulf.

The landscape the Mesopotamians knew looked very different from today. It is important to examine these changes in landscape to understand the story of Mesopotamia. Both the Euphrates and the Tigris flowed along different routes, much closer together (see map). The Euphrates River was divided into branches, and many towns were built along its banks. However, the Euphrates now flows farther west than it did in Mesopotamian times, and the Tigris has moved farther to the east.

Another reason why the landscape has changed is because of the sediment deposited at the head of the Persian Gulf by the two rivers. In Mesopotamian times the coastline of the Persian Gulf reached farther north, and the Euphrates and Tigris flowed straight to the gulf. However, over the past 5,000 years, the rivers have dropped so much sediment

A CLOSER LOOK

Between the Euphrates and Tigris rivers lies the floodplain. It has a hot and arid climate. Ruins of ancient towns and cities stand isolated on the floodplain—but in Mesopotamian times many of these settlements were on the banks of the Euphrates, linked together by this great river. As the course of the river changed, the old towns of Mesopotamia became stranded on the floodplain, far from the river's life-giving water.

into the Persian Gulf that it has become silted up, and the coastline has been pushed south. The open sea is now about 155 miles (250 km) farther away from the ancient cities of southern Mesopotamia than it was in Mesopotamian times.

Mesopotamia is often called "the cradle of civilization." Western civilization traces its very beginnings to Mesopotamia, and to the people who lived there. This was where some of the world's first experiments in agriculture and irrigation were carried out, where writing was invented, where the wheel was first used, where mathematics was born, and where the world's first cities were built.

ANCIENT PEOPLES OF MESOPOTAMIA

People	Where they lived	When they lived	Main town
Hunter-gatherers and first farmers	Along the Euphrates and Tigris rivers	10,000–3700 B.C.	—
First town dwellers	Southern Mesopotamia	3700–2900 B.C.	Uruk
Sumerians	In Sumer (southern Mesopotamia)	2900–2330 B.C.	Ur
Akkadians	In Akkad (northern Mesopotamia)	2334–2193 B.C.	Agade
Third Dynasty of Ur	Sumer and Akkad	2112–2004 B.C.	Ur
Amorites	Sumer	2004–1792 B.C.	—
Babylonians	In Babylonia (the area that used to be Akkad)	1792–1595 B.C.	Babylon
Kassites	In Babylonia	1595–1365 B.C.	Babylon
Assyrians	In Assyria (northern Iraq and southern Turkey)	1365–629 B.C.	Nimrud, then Nineveh
Chaldeans	In Chaldea (southern Iraq and Kuwait)	625–539 B.C.	Babylon

Although other peoples lived in Mesopotamia in the period covered by this book, this list shows which groups are looked at in detail.

FROM HUNTERS TO FARMERS

A good starting point for the story of Mesopotamia is with the ending of the last Ice Age, which scientists usually date to about 12,000 years ago. At this time in the Middle East, the climate began to warm up and rainfall increased. Trees of the forest, such as cedar, juniper, oak, and pine, liked the warmer, moister conditions and began to colonize the high ground. The lowland area, through which the Euphrates and Tigris rivers flowed, consisted of treeless grassland (steppe) in the north and desert in the south.

The region was home to many species of animals. Herds of gazelles, fallow deer, asses, and aurochs

The Asiatic mouflon is the ancestor of the domesticated sheep.

(large wild oxen with horns) grazed the grasslands. Deer, Asiatic mouflon (wild sheep), and Bezoar goats lived in the mountains, and boars in the marsh country. These animals were preyed on by carnivores, such as jackals, wolves, bears, lynxes, hyenas, cheetahs, leopards, tigers, and lions. There were also smaller animals including foxes, hares, hedgehogs, tortoises, snakes, lizards, and frogs. Fish and shellfish lived in lakes and in the Persian Gulf. Ostriches, partridges, ducks, and geese were just some of the region's many birds.

It was into this environment that small bands of wandering hunter-gatherers came, attracted by the area's plentiful supplies of edible plants and animals, and good sources of fresh water to drink.

THE HUNTER-GATHERERS

The hunter-gatherers of the Fertile Crescent led the life of nomads. They were wanderers who drifted across the landscape from one temporary campsite to the next. They moved around in small groups, which were probably based around family units, hunting animals and gathering plants.

Evidence for prehistoric hunter-gatherers in the Fertile Crescent is hard to find. The very nature of their unsettled, wandering lifestyles means they have left few recognizable marks on the landscape. What we can say about them is based on studying hunter-gatherer communities of recent times.

No doubt the hunter-gatherers of these ancient lands had a great understanding of the animals and plants around them. Perhaps they chose to hunt only mature, male animals, leaving young animals to grow and females to bear young. They would have observed which wild grasses produced the best seed heads. Perhaps each group returned at the same time each year to a particular area on the grassy plain that they regarded as "their patch," eager to gather its abundant grass seeds. Perhaps one year there was a bumper crop, so they stayed weeks or months instead of the usual few days, enjoying nature's harvest. And maybe this was the moment of change—one of the greatest turning-points in the history of humankind—when hunter-gatherers in the Fertile Crescent realized that nature could be controlled. As they began to domesticate plants and animals, they slowly gave up their nomadic lifestyle, settling in villages and working on the land as farmers.

DOMESTICATING PLANTS

Among the many different kinds of wild grass that grew in this area were einkorn and emmer wheat. They played an important role in the development of early farming.

Einkorn and emmer produced large seed heads, packed with good-sized grains. The first farmers gathered the grains of these two plants in the wild, in preference to plants that produced fewer seeds. However, both einkorn and emmer suffered from brittle ears that snapped easily, and both shed their grains quickly. Neither was particularly good for growing as a crop. Then, at some point, wild emmer wheat crossbred with wild goat grass. The resulting mixture, known as a hybrid, was a plant with tough ears that held on to its grains. When the first farmers realized the advantages of the hybrid plant, they chose it as their main crop.

With each year that passed, the hybrid emmer crop produced more

This arc-shaped area is known as the Fertile Crescent.

Map key:
- N
- TURKEY
- MESOPOTAMIA
- Tigris River
- SYRIA
- IRAQ
- IRAN
- Upper Sea (Mediterranean Sea)
- Euphrates River
- Jericho
- JORDAN
- EGYPT
- Lower Sea (Persian Gulf)
- **Key** — Area of Fertile Crescent
- 0   300m
- 0   300km

A CLOSER LOOK

In 1916, the American archaeologist, James Breasted, coined the term "Fertile Crescent." He noticed that a crescent-shaped area of land extended along the valley of the Euphrates and Tigris rivers, west to the shores of the Mediterranean Sea, then south to Egypt. It was an area characterized by dry summers and rainy winters, where the wild ancestors of wheat and barley grew, and where wild sheep and goats lived. It was here, within this broad arc of land, that the right conditions existed for the first experiments in food production to take place, some time around 9000 B.C.

People gather the wheat harvest along the banks of the Euphrates today—a scene little changed in thousands of years.

and better grains of wheat. By weeding out the weakest plants and leaving only the strongest to grow, farmers turned a wild plant into a domesticated one. They gained control of nature and were able to produce more food.

Other plants domesticated by farmers in the Fertile Crescent were barley, peas, lentils, carrots, turnips, and leeks. The cultivation of all these plants began to happen from about 9000 B.C. onward.

DOMESTICATING ANIMALS

At about the same time that the first farmers of this area were domesticating plants, the long process of taming wild animals to work for humankind had begun.

Young animals were taken from the wild and were raised to provide a guaranteed supply of meat and milk. As they produced their young, their numbers increased. The next step in the process of domesticating animals was when people realized that large numbers of animals could be kept together in flocks and herds. Large, aggressive animals were killed off before they became too dangerous, and before they could breed. By doing this over a long period of time, wild animals evolved into domesticated breeds that were smaller and more docile than their wild ancestors.

Probably the world's first domesticated animal was the dog. It was descended from the wolf, and was chosen to live and work with humans because of its suitability for hunting other animals. By around 7000 B.C., other Middle Eastern animals had evolved from their wild ancestors into domesticated breeds: the goat from the wild Bezoar goat, the sheep from the Asiatic mouflon (a wild sheep with curved horns and a woolly coat), the pig from the wild boar, the cow from the aurochs (a large wild ox with horns), and the cat from the wild cat. By about 2000 B.C., the donkey and the horse were domesticated, too.

THE FIRST VILLAGES

Humankind had taken two great steps along the path to civilization. People in the Fertile Crescent had learned how to grow crops and how to keep animals. The conditions were now right for an even greater step to be taken. Instead of living in temporary campsites, people began to build permanent places in which to live. These places were the world's first villages, the most ancient of which is about 11,000 years old.

Sheep are an important part of people's livelihoods in the Middle East today, just as they were 9,000 years ago.

As people settled in villages, the population began to increase. New tools were invented to help farmers with their crops, such as sickles for reaping wheat and barley, and plows to till the fields. People discovered how to build ovens in which to bake bread, and from this invention came the idea of baking clay to make pottery.

People learned how to extract linen thread from the flax plant. They spun flax and wool, weaving them into cloth for clothes, bedding, and sails. They found out that beer could be made from barley, and wine from grapes. Since there was no longer any need for people to move from campsite to campsite, as they had done before they lived in villages, they began to acquire possessions, such as furniture.

This skull comes from the town of Jericho in Jordan, one of the world's earliest farming communities, c. 9000 B.C. The inhabitants of Jericho worshiped their ancestors, decorating their skulls with painted clay and shells.

Another key stage in the development of civilization is the concept of trading goods over a wide area. As villagers produced more grain than they could use themselves, or made more pots than they needed, they traded the surplus for goods that they could not produce themselves. These goods included shells and semiprecious stones that were used to make necklaces, and obsidian, a black volcanic glass, that was used to make sharp cutting tools. Obsidian came from the area around Lake Van, in present-day Turkey, but it was widely traded among the first farming villages of the Middle East. We know this because cutting tools made from obsidian have been found throughout the Middle East—some more than 620 miles (1,000 km) from Lake Van.

FROM VILLAGES TO EMPIRES

The first villages in Mesopotamia were built in areas where there was enough rainfall for crops to grow and enough pasture for farm animals to graze. At first, villages were confined to the grassy northern part of Mesopotamia where there was frequent rainfall. But from about 6500 B.C. onward, villages began to appear in southern Mesopotamia. They stood on the fertile floodplain between the Euphrates and Tigris rivers—an area of low rainfall where it was essential for farmers to dig irrigation canals to take water to their crops.

The villages of this early period, whether they were built in the north or in the south of Mesopotamia, existed in the prehistoric period—the time before the invention of writing. Because of this we do not know what the people called themselves.

THE UBAID CULTURE

Ubaid is the name used by archaeologists for a culture that flourished for about 2,800 years,

A CLOSER LOOK

Archaeologists have invented names for the groups of people (called cultures) who lived in Mesopotamia before the invention of writing. Each group of people had a distinctive style of pottery, which is how archaeologists tell them apart:

Culture	Flourished	Built their villages in
Hassuna	6500–6000 B.C.	Northern Mesopotamia
Samarra	6200–5700 B.C.	Northern Mesopotamia
Halaf	6000–5100 B.C.	Northern Mesopotamia
Ubaid	6500–3700 B.C.	Southern Mesopotamia
Uruk	3700–2900 B.C.	Southern Mesopotamia

from 6500 B.C. to 3700 B.C. The name comes from Tell el-Ubaid, the modern name of an ancient village. The Ubaid people built their villages in the south of Mesopotamia, in the marshes at the head of the Persian Gulf. Their houses were made from bricks of mud, baked hard by the sun. Farmers irrigated their wheat and barley crops by building canals that channeled water from the Euphrates, especially when the river was swollen with floodwater in the spring. Farmers also kept sheep, goats, and pigs. Fishermen fished in the marshes and at sea. Ubaid potters made white pots painted with bold patterns, besides pottery figurines.

Farmers of the Ubaid villages mastered the food production process and were able to supply enough food to sustain an increasing population. Their craftworkers perfected the use of clay, copper, and stone. Their merchants traded goods with other villages. Religion played a growing part in everyday life, and no doubt each village had someone who was seen as its leader. Under these circumstances the right conditions existed for the world's first towns to emerge.

URUK—AN EARLY TOWN

Uruk is in southern Mesopotamia. In ancient times it was on the banks of the Euphrates. Uruk is

This pottery figure of a bull was made by people of the Ubaid culture, c. 4000 B.C.

important because it was one of the first towns in Mesopotamia, with a population of as many as 50,000 people.

There were three main reasons why Uruk grew so big: it controlled a vast amount of agricultural land, it was close to trade routes, and it occupied a good position close to the Euphrates. For all these reasons, people were attracted to Uruk. As more people settled in the town, it spread out across the plain until it covered 1,235 acres (500 ha) of land—bigger than Rome under the Roman emperors.

Not only was Uruk one of the first towns, but it was here that Mesopotamian culture began to emerge from its prehistoric period. Archaeologists have found more than 5,000 clay tablets at Uruk on which pictures of animals and wheat are marked. Next to the pictures are signs that represent numbers. This shows that the people of Uruk had invented a method of recording numbers of animals and amounts of crops. (See page 46.)

The decorated box known as the "Royal Standard of Ur" was probably the sounding box of a musical instrument, such as a lyre. On this side are scenes from everyday Sumerian life. On the reverse are scenes of war. (See page 45.)

SUMER AND THE SUMERIANS

From about 3000 B.C. onward, the changes that had transformed Uruk into a town were copied throughout southern Mesopotamia. Villages became towns, and towns became cities. This southern region was called Sumer, and its dark-haired, fair-skinned inhabitants were the Sumerians.

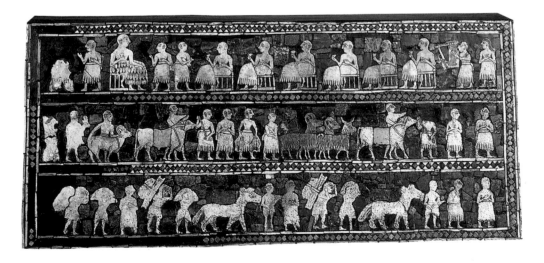

As the Sumerian cities grew, so a system of government developed. (See page 26.) Each city was ruled by a king and controlled the land immediately around it. Sumer became divided into a patchwork of small city-states, the most important of which was the city of Ur. (See page 32.) Palaces and temples were built in the towns, and high walls were put around them for protection from flooding and attack. Most significantly of all, the Sumerians invented writing. (See page 46.)

AKKAD AND THE AKKADIANS

This map shows the lands of Sumer and Akkad and their major cities. The capital city of the Akkadian Empire, called Agade, may lie close to Baghdad, the modern capital of Iraq.

While Sumerian cities flourished in the south, the northern part of Mesopotamia became home to a group of people called the Akkadians. They came from the west, possibly from what is now Arabia. Like their Sumerian neighbors, the Akkadian people built cities.

The Akkadians, led by Sargon the Great (see page 27), conquered Sumer. Under Sargon the two regions were united and, for the first time in its history, Mesopotamia was ruled as a single country.

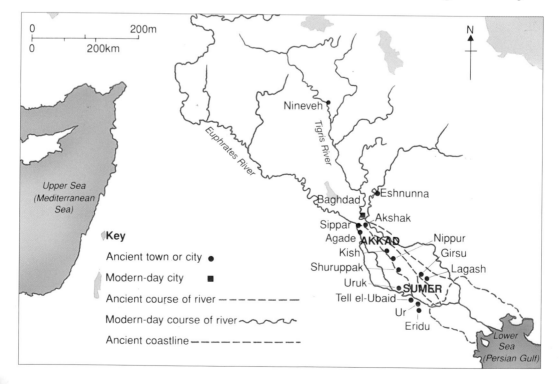

Key

Ancient town or city •

Modern-day city ■

Ancient course of river – – – – – –

Modern-day course of river ~~~~~

Ancient coastline – – – – – – –

A CLOSER LOOK
Language is one way of identifying different groups of people. Akkadian belongs to a group of languages spoken throughout the Middle East from about 3000 B.C. onward. The language used by the Sumerians did not belong to the same group. It died out as both a spoken and a written language when Akkadian became the main language of the region. Arabic and Hebrew (two languages spoken in the Middle East today) are both related to Akkadian. The writing of the Sumerians and Akkadians is called cuneiform. (See page 47.) Although it looks the same, experts who read it can tell that the Sumerians and Akkadians spoke different languages—just as English and French are different but both use the same alphabet for writing.

A statue of Gudea, the Sumerian king whose name meant "the Chosen One."

Akkadian became the official language for written documents, and it spread throughout Sumer, replacing the Sumerians' own language, which was eventually forgotten. The Akkadians adopted the Sumerian system of writing to write down their own language. They standardized weights and measures across the whole region. They also adopted some of the Sumerians' ideas about government (see page 26) and some of their gods and goddesses. (See page 38.)

The Akkadian Empire expanded across a large part of the Fertile Crescent, covering much of present-day Iran and Syria. At its greatest extent, it stretched from the Upper Sea (the Mediterranean Sea) in the north, to the Lower Sea (the Persian Gulf) in the south. But the Akkadians found it difficult to control their vast empire. There were constant uprisings among the people they ruled. Eventually, the Akkadians lost all their lands except for their capital city of Agade (sometimes known as Akkad).

SUMER AND THE THIRD DYNASTY OF UR

The end of the Akkadian Empire meant that the Sumerian cities in southern Mesopotamia were set free from foreign control, regaining their independence. For a short time the Sumerian culture flourished once more. Powerful new kings emerged to rule the old Sumerian cities. One of the first of these new rulers was Gudea, king of the Sumerian city of Lagash. He gained

The ziggurat at Ur, now partly restored, was dedicated to the moon god Nanna. It was originally about 82 feet (25 m) tall, with three platforms.

control over other cities in Sumer, revived old trade routes, and restored old temples.

Ur-Nammu was even more powerful than Gudea. He founded a dynasty (family) of rulers, known as the third Dynasty of Ur (2112–2004 B.C.) at the old Sumerian city of Ur. Ur-Nammu was proclaimed the "King of Sumer and Akkad." He restored temples and began to build tall towers with steps, known as ziggurats, beside them. (See page 32.) When Shulgi, Ur-Nammu's son, became king of Ur, he decided that the city should be the center of a great empire. His army conquered the peoples who lived to the north of Sumer and others who lived to the east. The empire of Ur became as large as the old empire of the Akkadians. But like the Akkadians before them, the Sumerian kings of Ur found it difficult to control their empire. One by one, the conquered cities broke free. Ur's power decreased and, in 2004 B.C., the city was invaded. Ibbi-Sin, the last Sumerian king, was led away in captivity, never to return. The great days of Ur were over.

THE AMORITE KINGDOMS

As the Third Dynasty of Ur collapsed, Mesopotamia and the Fertile Crescent entered a period of unrest. Groups of people moved across the region in search of safe places to live. The Amorites made up one of these groups. They came from somewhere west of Mesopotamia, perhaps from an area that now belongs to Syria.

The Amorites settled in Mesopotamia and took control of the Sumerian cities. Under the Amorites each city was ruled by a king. Mesopotamia was no longer part of a large empire. It was broken up into small kingdoms that were often in conflict with each other.

Hammurabi, king of Babylon. He is wearing a royal headdress.

THE RISE AND FALL OF BABYLON

Babylon began as a small town in central Mesopotamia, on the banks of the Euphrates. In 1894 B.C. it was captured by an Amorite chief called Sumu-abum. Babylon became the capital of his kingdom, and he became the first king in a long line of rulers. One of the descendants of Sumu-abum was a king called Hammurabi.

Hammurabi became king of Babylon in 1792 B.C. He established Babylon as the greatest city in the Middle East. Hammurabi also conquered neighboring cities in north and south Mesopotamia, and Babylon became the capital of a new Mesopotamian empire. One of Hammurabi's most important acts was to draw up a set of laws that everyone in his empire had to follow. (See page 29.)

21

The kings who came after Hammurabi gradually lost control of his empire. Cities rebelled, and the empire became weak. Invaders called Kassites, who may have come from central Asia, moved into Mesopotamia and took cities that had belonged to Babylon. In 1595 B.C. a Kassite king, Agum-Kakrime, seized the throne of Babylon itself.

The Kassite kings ruled Babylon for 400 years. Though they were foreigners, the Kassites maintained Babylonian ways of life. They respected the Mesopotamian gods, which were different from their own, and rebuilt their temples. They kept Babylon as the region's capital. At Dur-Sharrukin, in the north of Mesopotamia, they built a major new city, close to the border with the neighboring kingdom of Assyria.

The Assyrian Empire reached its greatest extent in the early 700s B.C., when it stretched from the Upper Sea (Mediterranean Sea) to the Lower Sea (Persian Gulf).

THE RISE AND FALL OF ASSYRIA

In 1365 B.C., Ashuruballit I became king of Assyria—a region that today covers northern Iraq and part of Turkey. His capital city was Ashur, home of the god of the same name. The king's own name meant "Ashur has preserved life." Ashuruballit's reign

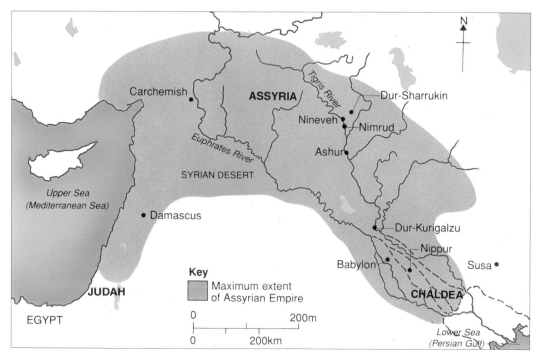

marked the start of Assyria's rise to power. He conquered part of a country called Mitanni that was north of Assyria, and he made contact with Egypt on the west.

Assyrian kings who came after Ashuruballit continued to add land to their growing empire. King Tukulti-Ninurta I captured Babylon, which he looted and burned. Part of the city's population was forced to leave. Under King Ashurnasirpal II, Assyria's empire reached as far as the Mediterranean Sea. He ruled over conquered peoples with great cruelty, forcing them to pay tribute, or money, each year. This tribute made Assyria rich. Ashurnasirpal II moved the capital city from Ashur, which was located at the southern edge of the country, to Nimrud, a town in the middle of Assyria on the east bank of the Tigris. He strengthened Nimrud with a wall 4.3 miles (7 km) long, enclosing some 890 acres (360 ha). The city had a population of tens of thousands. Within the city was a royal palace and temple complex where, for almost 200 years, the kings of Assyria lived.

Among the later kings was Sennacherib. He made the town of Nineveh the new capital of the Assyrian Empire. At 1,778 acres (720 ha), it covered twice as much land as Nimrud. King Sennacherib built canals to carry water to the city and its farmland, and a grand royal palace in the city center. It was decorated with painted and sculpted scenes. He put a park around the palace where he grew exotic plants. Sennacherib was a strong ruler. When his eldest son was murdered in Babylon, he destroyed the city. He dug canals to flood it and scattered the earth on which it stood across the empire.

The last of the great Assyrian kings was Ashurbanipal. His reign is sometimes seen as Assyria's "golden age"—a time when wonderful works of art were made, and when foreign ambassadors visited to pay their respects at

Ashurnasirpal II, king of Assyria. Long hair was fashionable for members of the royal court. In his left hand he holds a mace and in his right a sickle. The mace showed he was king. The sickle was used by the gods for fighting monsters.

These Assyrian soldiers are dressed in scale-armor. (See page 45.) Archers shoot arrows from behind tall, curved shields. A river flows at their feet.

the royal court. Nevertheless, it was during Ashurbanipal's reign that the Assyrian Empire began to collapse. Egypt, which had been conquered by the Assyrians, broke free. There was a rebellion in Babylon, and civil wars raged elsewhere. When Ashurbanipal died, in 629 B.C., the Assyrian Empire fell apart as invaders attacked it on all sides. Finally, when Nineveh itself was captured, the Assyrian Empire ended forever.

THE NEW BABYLONIAN EMPIRE

Chaldea was an ancient name for the marshy lands in the far south of Mesopotamia, at the head of the Persian Gulf—present-day southern Iraq and Kuwait. Tribes of settlers who arrived in this region became known as the Chaldeans. Exactly where they originally came from is a mystery.

At first, Chaldea was ruled over by Assyrian kings because it was part of their empire. But as the Assyrian Empire weakened, the Chaldean kings seized the moment and began to build an empire of

---

A CLOSER LOOK

Kings' names were carefully chosen, and each had a specific meaning.

● **Ashurnasirpal** meant "Ashur is the one who guards the heir to the throne."

● **Ashuruballit** meant "Ashur has preserved life."

● **Ashurbanipal** meant "Ashur is the creator of the heir to the throne."

● **Nabopolassar** meant "Nabu, guard the heir!"—Nabu was the Babylonian god of writing.

● **Nebuchadrezzar** meant "Nabu, guard the royal progeny!"

● **Sennacherib** meant "Sin has compensated for the death of the brothers"—possibly a reference to elder brothers of the king who had died young. Sin was the Assyrian moon god.

● **Tukulti-Ninurta** meant "My trust is Ninurta!"—Ninurta was the Assyrian god of war.

their own. It is called the New Babylonian Empire. When, in 625 B.C., King Nabopolassar captured Babylon from the Assyrians, the Chaldeans became the most powerful people in Mesopotamia.

It was Nabopolassar's son who made the greatest impression on the region. He was Nebuchadrezzar II —the king mentioned in the Bible as the destroyer of Jerusalem. He marched against the Egyptians and defeated them at the battle of Carchemish. Then, he rebuilt and enlarged Babylon, which became his capital. The seven-story ziggurat he built at Babylon is named the Tower of Babel in the Bible .

After Nebuchadrezzar II died, the New Babylonian Empire went into decline. The kings who came after him could not keep the empire together. Worst of all, a new power, that of the Persians, was rising in the east. (See page 58.)

This imaginative painting of the Tower of Babel is by the Dutch artist Pieter Brueghel the Elder (c. 1528–1569). He has made the ziggurat look more like a Roman amphitheater than a Mesopotamian mud-brick tower.

GOVERNMENT, SOCIETY, AND LAW

As cities grew out of villages, a method of running these new urban centers and organizing their populations was needed. The world's first system of government was created.

GOVERNMENT IN MESOPOTAMIA

The Sumerians devised the earliest form of government. Each of their cities controlled the land around it. Together, the city and its land are called a city-state. Sumer was a country of many city-states, all fiercely independent of one another.

The early days of Mesopotamian government are closely linked to religion. Each city had a temple, dedicated to the city's patron god or goddess. At the head of the city-state was a ruler whom the people believed was the god's representative on earth. He was also the city's chief priest, and he had three titles: *en*, meaning "the lord," indicating his religious role; *ensis*, meaning "prince" or "governor," indicating his role as leader; and *lugal*, meaning "the great man," indicating his position as leader of the army.

The ruler lived in a palace and had the power to make laws to govern his city. In the early days, he was elected by the people of the city, but as time went by the leader's role became more important. Instead of being an elected official, he began to pass the title on to his son, who passed it to his son, and so on. These

A CLOSER LOOK

In very broad terms, Mesopotamian society was divided into two groups of people—those who owned land and those who did not. By the time of Hammurabi (see page 21), three basic social classes had emerged: citizens (nobles and freemen who were landowners and heads of households); non-citizens (who did not own land); and slaves (prisoners of war and individuals who had let themselves be sold into slavery rather than face a life of poverty).

rulers were the first true kings. They believed they had been chosen by the gods, not by the people—so it was their god-given right to rule.

The system of government created by the Sumerians repeated itself throughout the history of Mesopotamia, as different cities rose to domination, led by powerful kings.

Could this be Sargon? Some people think this copper head of an Akkadian ruler depicts the great leader. The beard, hairstyle, and diadem (royal headband) indicate the figure is a king. The eyes, ears, and nose may have been deliberately damaged by people who came later, to show their supremacy over past leaders.

SARGON, KING OF AKKAD

Sargon's real name is not known. He took the name "Sargon" when he became king of Akkad. Sargon (reigned 2334–2279 B.C.) was the greatest of the Akkadian kings. Very little is known about his early life. According to legend, he was the son of a priestess. Soon after he was born she placed him in a reed basket that she cast to float freely on the Euphrates. Baby Sargon was found by a gardener, who raised him as his own son.

As a young man, Sargon worked for the king of Kish, a leading city. He was appointed the king's "cup-bearer," an important position at the royal court. During a revolt Sargon overthrew the king and seized power for himself. It is from this time on that he called himself Sargon, meaning "True King" or "Legitimate King." It was his way of emphasizing that people should accept no one else except him as their king. Sargon built a new capital city, named Agade.

Sargon was a great military leader. His army conquered the land of Sumer to the south, and when its cities came under his control, he assumed the title "King of the Land," in addition to his other titles "King of Akkad" and "King of Kish."

To strengthen his position in Sumer, he weakened the conquered cities of Sumer by destroying their defensive walls, and he placed his own officials in charge of them. For the first time in the history of Mesopotamia, the whole area was ruled as one land, because Sargon had united the countries of Akkad and Sumer.

To the north he conquered lands as far as the Mediterranean Sea. Cities were looted and their valuables were taken back to Sargon's capital. He took control of supply routes, and his empire grew wealthy. Merchant ships brought pottery, bone ornaments, and beads in precious stones from the Indus Valley that lay across the Indian Ocean, from Oman in the Middle East, and from Bahrain and other islands in the Persian Gulf. An account says that, "5,400 men ate bread daily before Sargon" —an indication of the size of his court, its officials, and merchant visitors. After reigning for 56 years Sargon died, either of old age, or in a revolt of one of the peoples he had conquered.

LAW IN MESOPOTAMIA

One of the most important duties of a Mesopotamian king was the passing of laws. Laws were necessary to rule a country successfully, and from early on in the history of Mesopotamia, collections of laws were issued.

The earliest known collection of laws dates from the time of Ur-Nammu, a powerful Sumerian king who founded the Third Dynasty of Ur. (See page 20.) His laws were written down in about 2100 B.C.— although they had probably been in use for very many years before this time. Only 28 of Ur-Nammu's laws are known today. They impose fines on guilty people. For example, one law says: "If a man has severed with a weapon the bones of another man, he shall pay one mina of silver" (a *mina* was a unit of weight. (See page 55.)

Under Sumerian law, a person accused of a crime was sent for trial before a panel of judges, who were elders chosen from the community. Witnesses had

Hammurabi's laws were inscribed in cuneiform on tall stones. On this example, Hammurabi stands before Shamash, the god of justice, who is telling the king to bring law and order to the land.

to tell the truth—just as in a modern court. The Sumerian system of law seems to have been a fair one. In fact many systems that came later were based upon it.

THE LAW CODE OF HAMMURABI

Hammurabi, king of Babylon, reigned from 1792 B.C. to 1750 B.C. He was a great organizer, and he paid close attention to how Babylon and its empire was run. He made sure the city's irrigation canals worked well, and he improved the calendar in order to keep it synchronized with the seasons. (See page 57.) However, Hammurabi's most famous act was the creation of a code of laws, designed to prevent the strong from taking advantage of the weak. It is the most famous list of Mesopotamian laws to have survived.

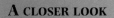

Hammurabi devised a list of 282 laws, some of which were based on the older Sumerian ones. They were organized into sections dealing with the family, work, property, land, prices and wages, slavery and trade. In the introduction to the list, Hammurabi explained how his system of law was intended to work. His wish was to "proclaim law throughout the land, eliminate what is bad, and prevent the

A CLOSER LOOK

Hammurabi's laws were carved on stones displayed throughout his empire. People referred to them to find out the punishment for a crime. Here are four of Hammurabi's 282 laws:

● If a man has accused another man and has brought a charge of murder against him, but has not proved it, his accuser shall be put to death.

● If a son has struck his father, they shall cut off his hand.

● If a man has put out the eye of another man, they shall put out his eye.

● If a builder has built a house for a man but has not made his work strong, with the result that the house falls down and kills the owner, the builder shall be put to death.

Laws such as these introduced the idea of retribution, which was where a person could legally "get even" with someone who had wronged them. Other laws handed out fines as punishments, as had been the custom under Sumerian law.

strong from oppressing the weak." It established a legal system in Mesopotamia for centuries to come.

ASHURBANIPAL, KING OF ASSYRIA

Ashurbanipal (reigned 668–629 B.C.) was a military leader and a scholar. He could read and write, and solve complex mathematical problems. But his main claim to fame rests with his eagerness to preserve Mesopotamian culture. During his reign, Ashurbanipal created a large library of cuneiform texts of all sorts, which he housed at Nineveh, his capital. (See page 34.) He sent collectors to search the temples of Mesopotamia for works of literature and magic, scientific writings, and medical reports, all of which were taken back to his library. Some of the texts were already old even in Ashurbanipal's time, dating back 2,000 years to the beginning of writing. When archaeologists discovered Ashurbanipal's library in the 1800s, its vast store of 20,000 clay tablets shed new light not only on the history of Assyria, but also on the civilizations of Sumer and Akkad. Had Ashurbanipal not collected these ancient writings, we would know far less about the history of Mesopotamia.

The Assyrian Empire reached its greatest extent under Ashurbanipal. He conquered Egypt, then raided the country of the Elamites (present-day Iran), where he ransacked Susa, the capital city. The temples of Susa were destroyed, booty was taken, and the land was sowed with salt so that nothing would grow. However, despite these military victories, the end of Ashurbanipal's reign was marked by the start of the collapse of the Assyrian Empire. Within 20 years of his death the empire had broken up and was lost forever.

This relief carving shows Ashurbanipal carrying a basket of earth from which the first mud-brick for a new temple at Babylon was to be made.

NEBUCHADREZZAR II, KING OF CHALDEA

Nebuchadrezzar II (reigned 604–562 B.C.) was the most important of the Chaldean kings, and one of the most famous figures in ancient history. His exploits are written about in the Bible, but he is best remembered as the builder of the Hanging Gardens of Babylon (see pages 35–36), and for his relations with the Jews.

The Jewish Kingdom of Judah lay between two great powers—Egypt and Babylonia. The Jews were unable to remain either independent or neutral; if they joined one side, they would be attacked by the other. When the Jewish king, Jehoiakim, turned against Babylon and stopped paying taxes, Nebuchadrezzar marched to Jerusalem and captured the city, in 597 B.C. Jehoiakim died, but Nebuchadrezzar wanted to exact punishment on the inhabitants of Jerusalem for their rebellious behavior. The defeated royal family, officials, soldiers, and craftworkers were all taken back to Babylon in chains. As many as 10,000 Jews may have been taken into captivity in Babylon.

Nebuchadrezzar destroys Jerusalem, as pictured by an artist in the early 1800s.

Ten years later there was a second uprising in Jerusalem. This time, after a siege lasting 18 months, Nebuchadrezzar destroyed the city, burning its temple and palace to the ground. The story of the fall of Jerusalem, and the part played by Nebuchadrezzar, is told in the Old Testament of the Bible by the prophet Jeremiah.

CITIES OF MESOPOTAMIA

Ur began as a village in about 4500 B.C. Over the next 2,000 years it mushroomed into a great, oval-shaped, walled city, covering some 148 acres (60 ha). By about 2500 B.C., it had become Sumer's leading city, with a population of about 20,000 people. Within its walls was a maze of narrow streets and winding alleys, packed with houses, stores, and markets. The city center was dominated by a massive temple complex, the centerpiece of which was a mud-brick ziggurat. (See box.)

Like other Sumerian cities built on the dry plain of southern Mesopotamia, Ur needed an adequate water supply—both for its population and for the patchwork of farmers' fields that surrounded it

Ziggurats were the center of religious life in every Mesopotamian city. A ziggurat was seen as a link between heaven and earth. The word "ziggurat" means "to build high." It comes from the word *ziqquratum*—a word used by the Babylonians. A ziggurat was a pyramid-shaped tower of several flat platforms, built one on top of the other. The platforms were reached by ramps and staircases. The entire structure was made from millions of sun-dried mud-bricks, held together with wooden beams and reed matting. Some of the outer bricks were glazed in bright colors. At the top of the ziggurat, was a small temple, dedicated to the city's god. There was a constant coming and going of priests, temple officials, worshipers, and slaves.

The partially restored ziggurat at Ur.

on all sides. The city was served by a canal, looping around it and linking it to the Euphrates. A network of ditches branched off from the canal, taking water to the fields of wheat, barley, onions, and leeks out on the plain. The city's two harbors were shelters for boats that brought foreign merchants from the island of Dilmun (present-day Bahrain), and elsewhere, to trade with the Sumerians.

THE ROYAL CEMETERY OF UR

The British archaeologist Leonard Woolley (1880–1960) excavated at Ur in the 1920s and 1930s. Beneath a thick layer of river silt, he found a cemetery where more than 2,500 Sumerians were buried. Commoners lay in simple graves, but 16 members of the Sumerian royal family were buried in deep tombs, packed with grave goods, that Woolley called the "Royal Cemetery."

What surprised and shocked Woolley and his team of excavators was the discovery that each ruler had been buried with their servants, soldiers, and musicians. The preparation for a mass burial was carefully worked out. First, a long, sloping shaft was dug down to a pit that would serve as the burial chamber. The chamber was filled with valuable offerings. Then, the body of the ruler was placed

This Sumerian board game came from the "Royal Cemetery" at Ur. It was made in c. 2600 B.C. Two players moved pieces around the board in a race.

on a wooden platform inside the chamber, together with the bodies of his closest attendants, each of whom had drunk poison. The burial chamber was sealed, and a procession of guards with daggers, musicians with lyres, grooms with ox-drawn chariots, soldiers with spears, and women of the court, moved into the shaft. Each carried a small cup of poison. They were prepared to die for their late ruler, to carry on serving him in the life after death. The shaft was filled with soil. One royal grave contained the bodies of 74 attendants, 68 of whom were women. On discovering this mass grave, Woolley and his team of archaeologists dubbed it the "Great Death Pit." He could find no signs of resistance among those who had sacrificed their lives—evidence which suggests that the Sumerians would obey their rulers and gods to the grave.

Attendants sacrificed in the Great Death Pit at Ur went to their deaths dressed in expensive clothes. Many of the women wore headdresses of gold and semiprecious stones.

NINEVEH, AN ASSYRIAN CITY

Like Ur, the city of Nineveh began as a village in the prehistoric period from about 6000 B.C. onward. More than 5,000 years later, the Assyrian king Sennacherib chose Nineveh as his capital, by which time it had grown into a major city covering more than 1,730 acres (700 ha). If the Biblical prophet Jonah is to be believed, at that time Nineveh had a population of 120,000.

King Sennacherib improved the water supply to Nineveh and the surrounding farmland by constructing canals and an aqueduct. At the center of the town, he built a magnificent palace that he called "The Palace Without Rival." It was both the home of the Assyrian royal family and the center of government. Its rooms were lined with painted and sculpted stone reliefs showing scenes of the king

As a young man, Henry Layard traveled throughout the Middle East. Here, aged 26, he is dressed as a tribesman from Iran.

defeating his enemies during the siege of Lachish, a town in the Jewish Kingdom of Judah. The siege is described in the Bible, and the images on the walls of Sennacherib's palace are eyewitness accounts of the actions of the Assyrian army, 2,700 years ago.

Around the outside of Sennacherib's palace a park was laid out, filled with unusual plants and animals brought from distant lands. But it was Sennacherib's grandson, Ashurbanipal, who gave Nineveh its greatest legacy—a library in which he housed the knowledge of Mesopotamia. (See page 30.)

French archaeologists, led by doctor and explorer, Paul Emile Botta (1802–70), had been digging at Nineveh for some years by the time a young British traveler arrived there in the 1840s. He was Austen Henry Layard (1817–94), and it was his work that uncovered the royal palaces of Sennacherib and Ashurbanipal. The French team had given up searching for them, but their failure did not deter Layard. His discoveries made him famous.

BABYLON, A CHALDEAN CITY

In the Akkadian language, Babylon was named "Bab-ilim," meaning "Gate of god." It was a holy city, the center of the god Marduk. The city was at its most splendid in the 500s B.C. during the time of the Chaldeans— a period that lasted less than 100 years following the collapse of the Assyrian Empire.

Nebuchadrezzar II (see page 31) transformed Babylon with an ambitious building program. Visitors entered the inner city through the Ishtar Gate, its colorful walls decorated with glazed bricks of blue, yellow, and white. Once inside the city, they passed the fabled Hanging Gardens, a rising terrace planted

A CLOSER LOOK

Tell el-Muqaiyir is the modern name for Ur, and Tell Kuyunjik is the name for Nineveh. In these, and other places, the Arabic word *tell* is a clue to the ancient origins of the settlement. It comes from the Babylonian word *tillum*, meaning "mound." Because the cities were occupied for thousands of years, they slowly rose above ground level as new buildings were built on the ruins of old ones. This activity created large mounds that rose many feet above ground level. It is into these mounds that archaeologists dig to uncover the remains of the ancient civilizations of Mesopotamia.

with trees and foliage, fed with water pumped from wells. From there they walked along the street known as "May the Enemy Not Have Victory" toward the city center, where the massive ziggurat to Marduk stood.

As many as 150,000 people of all nationalities may have lived in Babylon,—including thousands of Jews deported from Jerusalem. (See page 31.) At this time Babylon covered about 1,000 acres (405 ha). People lived in small mud-brick houses, which faced in from the street toward courtyards for privacy. All had flat roofs, and some had rooms for servants and slaves. The city was surrounded by a wall 10.6 miles (17 km) in circumference.

The Ishtar Gate was the main entrance into the inner city of Babylon. It was faced with glazed bricks showing images of lions and bulls.

A bull from the Ishtar Gate.

RELIGION AND MYTHOLOGY

Religion, and the ceremonies associated with it, played an important role in the lives of the Mesopotamians. Much of what we know about their beliefs, and their gods and goddesses, comes from reading stories they wrote. Many Mesopotamian myths (see page 39) have survived on clay tablets.

THE MESOPOTAMIAN UNIVERSE

The Mesopotamians thought that the universe was a sphere, organized into three parts—the sky, the earth, and the underworld. These three parts fit together like the parts of a jigsaw puzzle.

The sky was the upper part of the universe. People thought of it as a liquid mass. Fixed within it were the thousands of stars that gave light to the world. The earth was the very center of the universe. It was seen as a solid place completely surrounded by salty sea. People thought that both the earth and the sea floated on a vast lake of fresh water that burst through onto the surface of the land to make life-giving rivers and springs. The third part of the universe was the underworld—a dark place and the exact opposite of the sky. The Mesopotamians called

To protect a house and its occupants from demons, people buried small figurines of gods under the floor. This god has written on its arms, "Enter, spirit of peace!" and "Depart, spirit of evil!" Model dogs were also buried to act as guard dogs. They had names such as "Expeller of evil," "Catcher of the enemy," "Biter of his foe," and "Loud is his bark," and "Don't think, bite!"

it the "land of no return." It was where the dead went when they left the "land of the living."

Linking the three parts of the universe together were air and water. They were the sources of all life and fertility. They could move freely between the sky, the earth, and the underworld.

GODS AND GODDESSES

The Mesopotamians believed that humankind had been created to serve the gods. According to a story told by the Sumerians, people had been molded from clay by the gods. It was the duty of all people to work for the gods as their slaves. Failure to look after the gods could bring floods, drought, disease, or attacks from enemies.

Temples to the gods were built in all towns and cities. Inside these temples were statues and other images of the gods. People thought the gods actually lived inside their statues. This explains why the Mesopotamians treated statues of gods

Sumerian worshipers placed statues such as this one inside temples to pray to the gods on their behalf.

A CLOSER LOOK

There were hundreds of different gods and goddesses in Mesopotamia. Some were extremely popular and were worshiped at many towns and cities. Others were less popular and were followed in only one or two towns. An (also called Anu) was god of the sky, and his son, Enki (also called Ea), was god of the earth. His name meant "Lord Earth." Enki controlled the lake of fresh water on which the world floated. He was the master of wisdom, the god of arts and crafts, and the protector of humankind. Another son of An was Enlil, whose name meant "Lord Wind." He controlled all life by bringing life-giving air for people and animals to breathe. He possessed the Tablet of Destiny that foretold the fate of humankind. He eventually became king of the gods. Marduk, son of Enki, became the main god of the Babylonians. Nanna (also called Sin) was the son of Enlil and, as the moon god, ruled over the calendar.

Adad, the weather god, controlled storms and rain, and Utu (also called Shamash) the sun god, gave light and heat to the world. Inanna (also called Ishtar) was the most important and feared goddess, whose name meant "Lady of Heaven." She was the goddess of love and war who had powers of life and death. Ninhursag was the great mother goddess whose name meant "Lady of the Mountain." Two other deities were Nabu, the god of scribes and writing, and Ninurta, the god of war and hunting.

and goddesses with great care and respect. The worst that could happen to a statue was that it might be captured and carried off by an enemy. When this happened, as it did from time to time, it was felt the god and his protecting presence had left the town, quite literally leaving it godless. The "good times" would return only when the god's statue was brought back.

A temple statue was made of wood, decorated with gold. At a secret ceremony, priests said prayers to bring the statue to life. From that moment on the god lived inside its statue. The statue stood on a pedestal inside the sanctuary, which was the temple's holiest room. Other statues in the sanctuary represented the god's family, his servants, and worshipers praying.

THE ART OF TELLING THE FUTURE

The Mesopotamians believed that it was possible to predict the future. The most widely practiced method of determining the future was by reading the stars, but other methods were used, too. Inspecting the entrails of a sacrificed sheep, interpreting dreams, noting the behavior of birds and other animals, and observing the directions taken by smoke from burning incense, or oil on water, were all used by priests to foretell events that would happen sometime in the future.

Natural phenomena, such as thunder, hail, rain, and earthquakes, were thought to be omens. They were sent by the gods to warn the king about danger to himself or the country. The Assyrians were such believers in these omens that they built weather stations where scribes recorded their observations on clay tablets. The tablets were sent to the king for interpretation by his priests.

MYTHS OF THE MESOPOTAMIANS

Many stories were told by the people of Mesopotamia about their gods and about how the world was created. The stories were written in cuneiform on clay tablets. (See page 49.) Many of these were stored in libraries at royal palaces, such as at Ashurbanipal's great library in Nineveh. When cuneiform was deciphered in the middle of the 1800s, scholars could read for themselves the myths of the Mesopotamians. What they read amazed them, because these myths cast new light on some of the stories that appear in the Old Testament of the Bible.

THE *EPIC OF GILGAMESH*

The *Epic of Gilgamesh* is the greatest of all Mesopotamian myths, written on 12 large clay tablets in about 3,000 lines of cuneiform. It came to light among the ruins of Ashurbanipal's library, built by him in the 600s B.C. But the story was already ancient by the time the Assyrian king added it to his collection of Mesopotamian literature.

In the story, Gilgamesh and his friend Enkidu set out to learn the secret of immortality. To begin with they think the way to live forever is by doing great deeds. In one adventure Enkidu kills the demon Humbaba, and in another Gilgamesh slays a bull sent to destroy the city of Uruk. But their bravery does not lead to eternal life, for Enlil, the king of the gods, decides that Enkidu must die as a punishment for killing Humbaba. The death of Enkidu teaches Gilgamesh an important lesson. That is no matter how heroic a man is, he remains a mortal whose fate lies in the hands of the gods. Gilgamesh's search for endless life leads him to Ut-napishtim, whose name means

In the Epic of Gilgamesh, *Enkidu kills the demon Humbaba. Images of this demon show his face made from the fatty entrails of a sacrificial animal.*

"I have found eternal life." Ut-napishtim explains to Gilgamesh that long ago Enlil sent a flood to destroy humankind. The god Enki took pity on Ut-napishtim and told him to build a great boat in which to save himself, his family, and all the living creatures of the world. On the seventh day of the flood Ut-napishtim first sent out a dove, and then a swallow. Unable to find a safe place to land, both returned to the boat. But when Ut-napishtim released a raven, and it did not return, he knew it must have found dry land. He offered sacrifices as thanks to the gods, and in return Enlil made him immortal, just like the gods themselves.

As for Gilgamesh, he never does discover the secret of immortality for himself, and so he returns to his home city of Uruk in the knowledge that, as a mere mortal, death is inevitable.

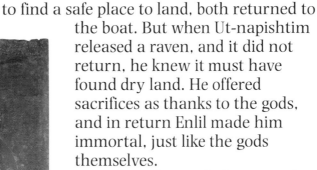

The hero Gilgamesh masters a lion. This huge statue is 15 ½ feet (4.7 m) tall.

A CLOSER LOOK

Is the Bible story of Noah, in Genesis, based on the Mesopotamian story of Ut-napishtim? In 1872, George Smith (1840–76) was working at the British Museum, London, joining together fragments of clay tablets found at Ashurbanipal's library at Nineveh. He came across the tablet with the story of Ut-napishtim and was stunned to read about a flood, a great ship and a dove. The similarity with the story of Noah was unmistakable. Experts believe that both the Ut-napishtim and Noah stories can trace their origins to a single flood story that was told in the ancient Middle East at least from the time of the Sumerians. Ut-napishtim and Noah are probably names for the same person.

EVERYDAY LIFE

The evidence for the everyday life of the people of Mesopotamia comes mainly from discoveries made by archaeologists. Objects found buried in the ground are used to increase our understanding about people's daily lives. However, so much evidence has not survived the passage of time that what we do know with any certainty is only a glimpse into the distant world of the Mesopotamians.

Bread made without yeast on sale in the Middle East today.

FOOD AND DRINK

Grain was made into flour, from which unleavened bread was baked. Because there was no yeast in the dough, loaves did not rise when baked, so they stayed quite flat. Bread was the staple food from the time of the Sumerians onward. Wheat and barley grains could also be softened and made into a kind of thick porridge. Other foods were onions, leeks, cucumbers, beans, garlic, and lentils. Milk, butter, and cheese came from goats and cattle. Dates were eaten fresh, dried, or pressed into a sweet-tasting syrup. Meat came from cattle and sheep. Fish was always popular, caught in rivers, pools, and from the sea.

The main drink was a low-alcohol beer, brewed from wheat or barley. Cuneiform texts refer to at least 19 different types of Mesopotamian beer. It could be flavored with dates, honey, and spices. Beer was a nutritious drink—a food in its own right. Everyone drank it, including children.

CLOTHING AND MAKEUP

During the Sumerian period, men went about bare-chested, dressed only in a type of kilt. Later on, this was replaced by a loose-fitting, shirtlike garment. Women wore long shawls and fitted dresses, their hair left loose or coiled around their heads. Both Sumerian men and women wore makeup, especially to emphasize their eyes. The mineral antimony provided a blue-black paint that was applied around the eyes and to the eyebrows and eyelashes. Women colored their lips and cheeks with red henna, smoothed their skin with pumice stone (a type of volcanic rock), took perfumed baths, and rubbed themselves with oils.

The gold and bead headdress of Queen Pu-Abi, from the Royal Cemetery of Ur. (See page 33.) The head is modeled on the skull of a Sumerian woman.

MUSIC

Among the thousands of clay tablets found in Mesopotamia, some are musical texts. They have been called the oldest examples of "sheet music" known to exist. When musicologists studied them in the 1970s, they discovered the music was for stringed instruments called lyres. One tablet, from Ugarit in northern Syria, turned out to be the words and music for the world's oldest song, written around 1400 B.C. It was a hymn to a Mesopotamian goddess, composed in a scale of seven notes played in harmony. Experts were surprised to discover that the hymn was in the "do, re, mi" scale of notes, which is the one used by many musicians today. Until this discovery it was thought that ancient music consisted of single, unharmonized notes. In 1974, musicians gave a performance of the Mesopotamian hymn from Ugarit—its first public performance for more than 3,300 years!

A reconstruction of a Sumerian lyre of about 2600 B.C.

WARFARE IN MESOPOTAMIA

Wars were fought throughout the long history of Mesopotamia. Cities attacked their neighbors, often in disputes over control of the valuable irrigation canals that brought water to them and their fields. In other wars, armies conquered the lands of their enemies, looted their cities, took the statues of their gods from their temples, and forced their populations into slavery. It was through military campaigns such as these that kings were able to build their empires.

This stele (an upright stone) records the battle victory of the Akkadian king Naram-Sin. With bow in hand, he leads his troops through wooded mountains. His horned cap is a symbol of his power.

Warfare in Mesopotamia reached a high point under the Assyrians, who had an army of up to 50,000 men. Assyrian soldiers wore pointed helmets and tunics, and fought with slings, bows and arrows, and spears. Their shields were made from wicker and leather. Some soldiers wore long robes covered with metal plates, which was an early form of armor. Horses were used for riding and for pulling chariots. At first, Assyrian chariots carried two men—one to drive and the other to fire arrows or throw spears. As time went by, chariots became larger and could carry four soldiers. Horses wore blinkers over their eyes and had bells attached to their harness straps. Breastplates made from bronze or leather hung down from their necks.

An Assyrian soldier's pointed helmet, made of iron.

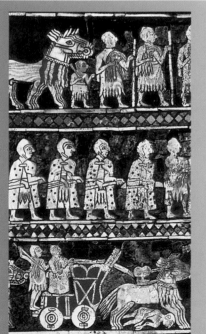

A CLOSER LOOK

The Sumerian army was well organized. Soldiers wore copper helmets, fought with spears and axes, and carried large rectangular shields. In some battles they used slow-moving, two-man chariots, pulled by donkeys. One side of the "Royal Standard of Ur," made in about 2600 B.C., shows the Sumerian army in detail. Part of the standard is shown here. At the bottom is a four-wheeled chariot. While the charioteer steers the vehicle over the body of a fallen enemy, his passenger throws spears. In the middle scene prisoners are being pushed along by soldiers carrying spears. In the top panel courtiers walked toward the king. Most Sumerian prisoners of war were executed. Any who were spared were kept as slaves.

The war side of the Standard of Ur.

ARTS AND CRAFTS

Like most other ancient civilizations, such as those of the Egyptians, Greeks, and Romans, the Mesopotamians possessed their own distinctive styles of art that can be recognized in their artifacts. Archaeologists use these cultural differences to help pinpoint places where objects were made, and to build up a dating framework into which historical events can be placed.

One of the world's first accounting documents, from c. 3200 B.C. The surface is divided into sections, in which there are pictographic signs, some representing numbers.

THE INVENTION OF WRITING

Writing started in Sumer, possibly at the town of Uruk, in about 3300 B.C. (See page 16.) This was a time of great change for the villages of southern Mesopotamia. They were growing into busy towns, and trade was emerging as an important part of their economy. People wanted to know how much grain or how many sheep were entering or leaving their stores and farms, so a method of keeping reliable records was needed. Writing was invented in order to record the business activities of farmers and merchants.

The first type of writing used pictures to represent objects or ideas. These are called ideographs. For example, a picture of a head meant "head" and two wavy

lines meant "water." Ideographs took time to write because each picture had to be drawn neatly and carefully. In order to write faster, original pictures with curves were gradually changed into forms that could be written with straight lines only.

WRITING ON CLAY

The Mesopotamians wrote mostly on small pieces of damp clay. Clay was easy to find and cheap to use. A piece of clay could be worked into a flat tablet that fit into the palm of the writer's hand. A tool called a stylus was used to write on the soft clay. It was made from the stem of a reed, or a piece of wood or bone. Its tip was gently pressed into the soft clay of the tablet to make small wedge-shaped impressions. After it had been written on, a clay tablet was left in the sun to dry, until it was hard.

Wedge-shaped, or cuneiform, writing on a clay tablet. It required skill both to write and read the mass of tiny impressions made by scribes on tablets like this.

When scribes discovered that a stylus with a blunt, wedge-shaped tip made a cleaner, sharper impression in clay, the system of picture writing began to change. In its place came the cuneiform script, made up of wedge-shaped marks. The word cuneiform comes from two Latin words: *cuneus* meaning "wedge" and *forma* meaning "shape."

Clay tablets were used for keeping everyday records and accounts, but they were not the only objects on which the Mesopotamians wrote. Cuneiform was also carved on to hard surfaces, such as stone and metal. Cuneiform became the main script of the ancient Middle East, and it was used

A CLOSER LOOK

When the first cuneiform inscription was published in Europe in the 1600s, it aroused little interest among scholars. They did not believe that the strange wedge-shaped marks were writing. One said they were experiments in making patterns using a triangular shape. Another said they were tracks made by birds! But as more examples of cuneiform were found, scholars realized they were dealing with a type of extinct writing—and so the race to decipher it began. The real breakthrough was made by a British army officer, Henry Rawlinson (1810–95). In the 1840s Rawlinson copied out a large cuneiform inscription carved high on the side of a cliff at Bisitun in western Iran. The same cuneiform inscription had been carved in three different languages (Old Persian, Elamite, and Babylonian). By studying them all, side-by-side, Rawlinson was able to work out what the signs said.

by the peoples of the region— the Sumerians, Akkadians, Babylonians, Assyrians, and Persians—for more than 3,000 years. The latest inscription written in cuneiform is dated to A.D. 75, after which time it went out of use.

CYLINDER SEALS

Cylinder seals were invented in Mesopotamia at about the same time as writing. They, too, came about because of the growth of the economy—in this case the need to establish the ownership of property. They were usually made from stone, but shell, ivory, and metal were also used. Their surfaces were engraved with intricate patterns, often of gods and animals. When rolled over damp clay they left an impression, or print, of the pattern of the engraving. This impression was a person's "signature," identifying him or her as the owner of property such as jars, baskets, and boxes. Seals protected a person's property, and owning a seal was a mark of prestige.

A cylinder seal (left) and its impression rolled on clay (right).

A CLOSER LOOK

Letters written in cuneiform on clay tablets were put inside envelopes made from clay. On the envelope was written the name and address of the person for whom the letter was intended. A cylinder seal was often rolled over the outside of the envelope, leaving a print of its pattern. When the letter arrived, the recipient checked to make sure the seal had not been broken—if it had then he or she knew that someone else had already opened the envelope and had probably read their private letter.

Letter

Clay envelope

LEARNING TO READ AND WRITE

People who could read and write (scribes) were highly thought of in Mesopotamian society—but learning cuneiform script was a long, hard process. As one scribe wrote to his son who wanted to follow in his father's footsteps, "Of all the human trades that exist on earth...none is more difficult than the art of the scribe."

Scribes were taught to read and write cuneiform in a school called an *edubba*, which literally means "tablet-house." There were more than 500 different cuneiform signs to memorize, and it took years before a scribe was fully trained. While he was learning cuneiform, a pupil at an *edubba* was called a "son of the tablet-house," and his teacher was the school "father." Pupils nearing the end of their training were called "elder brothers" and acted as both friends and bullies toward the younger pupils in the school. Elder brothers expected the younger pupils to give them presents (bribes). If they did not, then a beating was sure to follow.

The school day lasted from sunrise to sunset. Teaching was strict—pupils who did poorly were beaten with a rod. Pupils were taught science, literature, mathematics, and grammar. Mathematics was an important subject to master. (See page 55.)

49

Three different teachers taught it: a "scribe of accounting" (teaching arithmetical skills such as addition, subtraction, and division); a "scribe of measurement" (teaching skills of geometry and distance); and a "scribe of the field" (a surveyor who taught how to calculate areas of land).

Cuneiform signs were small and complicated, so pupils had to learn how to write neatly without making mistakes. This they did by copying out inscriptions time and time again. Pupils also had to learn words and phrases by heart, and took examinations to test their memory and knowledge.

POTTERY

The first pots made from baked clay were fashioned in the Fertile Crescent about 7000 B.C. They are some of the oldest ceramic vessels in the world, and their manufacture coincided with the development of village communities, where people lived in permanent settlements. (See page 13.)

As potters learned how to use clay, the range of pots they made increased. Pieces of broken pottery, or potsherds, are the commonest finds made by archaeologists and, as fired clay is virtually indestructible, it is possible to recreate whole pots from a jigsaw puzzle of fragments.

Mesopotamian pots included bowls, plates, saucers, and jars, in many sizes from small to large. At first pots were handmade, slowly built up from coils or slabs of clay which were pressed into shape. From about 4500 B.C., the potter's wheel was introduced, enabling potters to make pots with thinner sides and in more elaborate shapes.

Many pots were left undecorated. They came from the kiln in shades of red and black, the color of their bodies determined by how much, or how little, oxygen had been present during the firing process. Other pots were decorated in a variety of ways. Some were coated with a thin wash of liquid clay called slip, often in a contrasting color to the body of the pot. On some pots the slip was used like paint to make patterns on the surface of the vessel. When a pot's surface was burnished, or rubbed, with a wooden or bone tool, shiny patterns could be made as the clay became slightly compressed. Other techniques involved impressing unfired pots with stamps, or cutting into the surface.

Styles of pottery are linked to particular groups of people at different times. The style of a pot is used by archaeologists to determine when and where it was made, which is particularly important when studying the prehistoric communities that existed before writing.

WORKING IN STONE

The stonemason's art was highly developed in Mesopotamia. Stones such as alabaster, basalt, diorite, gypsum, jasper, and limestone were all used to make statues, cylinder seals, and, most notable of all, the scenes of hunts and battles carved on large stone slabs that lined the walls of Assyrian palaces.

Most Assyrian palace reliefs were carved between 870 B.C. and 620 B.C. The palaces, built from perishable mud-brick, contained painted rooms

This stone relief, a type of sculpture, shows soldiers escaping from Ashurnasirpal's army by swimming across the Euphrates River. They cross the river supported by inflated animal skins and head to the fort on the right.

51

with floors covered by carpets. Set against the walls were 6 1/2 foot- (2 m-) high panels of carved stone, depicting scenes that were themselves painted.

The most widely-used stone for palace reliefs was a form of gypsum, sometimes known as Mosul marble. (The modern town of Mosul lies on the right bank of the Tigris, opposite the ancient city of Nineveh.) Grayish-white in color and finely-grained, blocks were cut from the rock with iron saws. They were then split and shaped, and mounted on the palace walls. The carving was done once the stone was mounted.

The purpose of the palace reliefs was to create an impression of Assyrian power and might. Visitors who saw the reliefs could not fail to be impressed by their scale and grandeur, or to understand their political message—that the Assyrian king was all-powerful, and the Assyrian Empire was all-conquering.

To archaeologists, the images on the stones tell vivid stories about the people of the time: how they dressed, how they were organized, the wars they fought, the technology they possessed, and their religious beliefs. But a word of caution is needed. They also acted as a powerful means of distributing propaganda. A king could enhance his reputation by deliberately exaggerating his success in battle, changing the truth to suit his needs.

The helmet of King Meskalamdug, shaped like a wig, comes from the Royal Cemetery of Ur. It was beaten from a single sheet of gold, the hair pattern being stamped out from the inside in a technique called "chasing."

METALWORK

Copper was a valuable resource for the early Mesopotamians who used it to make tools, weapons, and decorative objects. The raw material (ore) for making copper was transported down the Euphrates from hills in the north to metalworkers who lived in the south.

When copper is mixed with tin, it forms an alloy called bronze. Bronze is harder than copper and made stronger tools and weapons that stayed sharp longer. The Sumerians made great use of bronze. They discovered it could be cast in clay or stone molds that enabled them to "mass produce" some items. Casting was used to make axes, daggers, and spearheads.

Of all metals, gold survives the best, and many examples of Mesopotamian goldwork have been found. A versatile metal, gold was put to many uses: jewelry, cups, and vases were made. Daggers, harps, lyres, and statues were covered with it or had pieces inlaid for decoration. Metalworkers found out how to make thin sheets of gold, and silver, by beating it out over flat stones. From this sheet metal, they shaped vessels with wide, open mouths, such as dishes and bowls.

Assyrian green glass vase from Nimrud, c. 750 B.C. It was made in a mold, then smoothed by grinding and polishing.

GLASS

The discovery of how to make glass, in about 1600 B.C., was one of the great achievements of the Mesopotamians. Glass had been made for several centuries before this time, but it was the accidental by-product of other processes, especially the smelting of copper and the firing of pottery. In both these cases, small glassy beads were formed as a waste product, and no doubt craftworkers wondered if this new material had any uses. By the middle of the 1000s B.C., they had learned how to make glass using silica from sand or ground-up pebbles of quartz.

SCIENCE AND TECHNOLOGY

The search for scientific knowledge was widespread among the civilizations of the Middle East. Fundamental principles of mathematics and astronomy were known. In medicine, doctors studied the human body and how to heal it. But probably the most significant aspect of Mesopotamian technology was the invention of the wheel.

THE WHEEL

The wheel was probably invented some time before 3200 B.C. The evidence for this comes from the early town of Uruk. Clay tablets with pictures of wheeled carts scratched on them have been found there. The first wheels were solid, made from two or three planks of wood shaped into disks held together with wooden or copper brackets. Solid wheels were in use for more than 1,000 years in Mesopotamia before lighter wheels with spokes were made, from around 2000 B.C. onward.

A Sumerian cart with solid wooden wheels, shown on the Royal Standard of Ur.

MATHEMATICS

The Sumerians were the first people to develop a system of arithmetic. The Sumerian system was adapted and improved by the Babylonians, and it spread throughout the ancient Middle East. Adding, subtracting, and multiplying were important skills when counting goods such as sacks of grain, or numbers of sheep and cattle.

The most widely used number system was based on counting in units of 60. This is called a sexagesimal system. Although 60 might seem a strange counting unit, it is in fact extremely practical because it can be divided exactly by 2, 3, 4, 5, 6, 10, 12, 15, 20, and 30, which makes many calculations quite simple. There was also another counting system, based on counting in tens, hundreds, and thousands, called a decimal system.

To help with calculations, people used multiplication tables. Other tables helped them with division, and with square roots and cube roots of numbers. Tables were written on clay tablets.

WEIGHTS AND MEASURES

Closely connected with counting was the system of weights and measures. This, too, was based on units of 60. In the Babylonian period, the basic weight was the *mina* (about 18 ounces or 500 g) which was subdivided into 60 *shekels*. Measures of length were based on the cubit or "elbow" (about 19.6 inches or 50 cm). The Babylonian "mile" was the equivalent of about 6.2 miles (10 km), which was the distance a person could walk in about two hours.

Assyrian bronze weights in the shape of lions. The largest was equal to 5 mina (about 88 ounces or 2.5 kg).

DOCTORS AND MEDICINE

The Mesopotamians believed that illnesses were caused by harmful demons inside a person's body. Some demons were said to cause diseases of the stomach, while others were blamed for illnesses of the limbs, head, or eyes. When a person became ill, they had a choice of two types of medical doctor—the *ashipu* and the *asu*. The *ashipu* was an expert in magic, somewhat like a sorcerer. The *asu* was the practical doctor, who treated patients with herbal remedies made from more than 100 different species of plants.

One of the most important roles of the *ashipu* was to diagnose a patient's illness by the use of magic. The *ashipu* decided which demon was causing the illness and whether it was the result of an error or sin committed by the patient. Once a diagnosis had been made, the *ashipu* began curing the patient by using magical charms and spells to drive out the harmful demon.

Patients who saw the *asu* received practical treatment. For cuts and wounds the *asu* applied ointments made from plants, spices, and animal fats, held on by bandages. The ointments had antiseptic qualities that worked like soaps to ward off infection from bacteria. If the patient had an internal illness, the *asu* gave them a potion to drink. It, too, was made from plant extracts, dissolved in beer, which probably made the medicine go down easier. The *asu* was also skilled in mending broken bones and in performing minor operations.

From the evidence so far found, most Mesopotamian doctors were men, though a single female doctor is known to have worked in Babylon. There may well have been other women doctors, too. Midwifery was certainly practiced exclusively by women doctors.

Gula, the goddess of medicine, surrounded by symbols of other gods

THE CALENDAR

Along with many other ancient civilizations, the Mesopotamians used a calendar based on the phases of the moon (new moon, crescent, half moon, waxing, and full moon). This is called a lunar calendar. Their year was divided into 12 months of 29 or 30 days each, and each month began when the new crescent moon was first sighted in the night sky. The problem with a calendar based on the lunar year is that it has 11 days fewer than a year based on the movement of the sun or 365 days. To make up the difference, the Mesopotamians added an extra month to their year, about every three years, to keep the lunar calendar synchronized with the solar (sun) calendar. Without this additional month, the seasons would begin to change at different times each year. Astronomers compiled lists predicting the future positions of the sun, the moon, and the planets. They were worked out for many years ahead, and were used to determine the beginning of months and years.

The oldest map in the world, from c. 600 B.C., puts Babylon at the center of everything, surrounded by neighboring lands (small circles) and the sea (large circle). The Euphrates is shown as a wide band running from top to bottom.

MAPS AND MAPMAKING

Clues as to how the Mesopotamians pictured the shape of the world exist in the form of maps marked out on clay. The so-called Babylonian "world map" is the oldest map in the world to depict the relative locations of neighboring countries. Dating from 600 B.C., it shows Babylon near the center of the world. The Euphrates River flows in a broad band across the world, and around are marked the countries of Assyria, Urartu (present-day Armenia), and parts of western Iran. Surrounding the land is the great circle of the Salt Sea, beyond which are marked regions where fabulous beasts were thought to live, and where the sun was not seen.

PERSIA—THE RISING NEW POWER

The revival of Babylon's fortunes under the Chaldean kings was short lived. (See page 24.) To the east of their New Babylonian Empire a power was growing that was to dominate the region for many centuries in the future.

The ruins of Persepolis lie in modern-day Iran. Persepolis is the Greek name for the city built by the Persian king, Darius. Many fine columned buildings stood at its center on a large stone platform that rose 49 feet (15 m) above the surrounding plain.

THE RISE OF THE PERSIANS

The country of Persis, the homeland of the Persians, lay east of Babylon, in present-day Iran. In 559 B.C., Cyrus became the Persian king. With his accession to the Persian royal throne, the balance of power in the Middle East changed. Cyrus waged war on his neighbors, the Medes, who had themselves been at war with the Assyrians. When he captured the city

A CLOSER LOOK

The empire created by Cyrus was strengthened by powerful leaders who came after him, chief of whom was Darius (reigned 522–486 B.C.). Darius is remembered for his military and administrative skills. It was during his reign that hostilities between the Persians and their western neighbors, the Greeks, intensified. He was the first Persian king to cross into Europe, extending the Persian Empire from present-day Bulgaria to Pakistan—the largest empire the world had yet seen. His son, Xerxes (reigned 486 to 465 B.C.), continued his father's military maneuvers against the Greeks, taking as many as 200,000 troops and 600 warships on a campaign that was ultimately to end in defeat at the battle of Salamis in 480 B.C. From this time on the Greeks gained the upper hand in the continual struggle for supremacy.

of Hamadan, the Medes' capital, he gained control of all their lands, from the Black Sea in the west as far as the Indus River valley in the east.

Cyrus then turned his attention toward the Lydians, whose land occupied much of present-day Turkey. He added their country to his empire after defeating them in battle in 547 B.C. His conquest of Lydia pushed the western boundary of the Persian Empire as far as the shores of the Mediterranean and Aegean seas, bringing him into hostile contact with the Greek world for the first time. Cyrus' next conquest was Mesopotamia itself. On October 23, 539 B.C., Cyrus and his Persian army entered the city of Babylon. The Babylonians were celebrating a festival and offered little or no resistance to the invaders. Cyrus proclaimed himself "King of the world— King of Babylon, King of Sumer and Akkad."

Cyrus was a wise and righteous ruler. He allowed the Jews exiled in Babylon by Nebuchadrezzar to return to their home city of Jerusalem (see page 31), a triumph for which he is praised in the Bible, in the Old Testament book of Isaiah. The Greek historians Herodotus and Xenophon also wrote about his life in legendary terms.

This procession of conquering soldiers from the Persian army is carved on a stairway leading to the palace of Darius at Persepolis.

TIMELINE

Most of the dates in this list can only be given approximately.

B.C.

c. 14,000	The last Ice Age ends. Rainfall and temperature increases.
c. 10,000	Hunter-gatherers start to harvest wild grains.
c. 9000	Domestication of plants and animals begins.
c. 9000	Jericho, the world's oldest town, is settled.
c. 7000	First pottery made in the Fertile Crescent.
c. 6500	The first villages appear in southern Mesopotamia.
c. 4500	First use of plow in Mesopotamia.
c. 3700	Uruk, the first town in Mesopotamia emerges.
c. 3300	Picture writing appears.
c. 3200	The wheel is invented.
c. 3100	Cuneiform script develops.
c. 2900–c. 2300	The Sumerian civilization flourishes in southern Mesopotamia.
c. 2600	The Royal Cemetery is in use at Ur, where rulers and nobles were buried with valuable grave goods and their sacrificed attendants.
c. 2600	First use of a four-wheeled war wagon.
c. 2330–c. 2200	The Akkadian civilization flourishes in northern Mesopotamia.
2334–2279	Reign of Sargon, king of Akkad.
2112–2004	The time of the Third Dynasty of Ur.
2004–1792	The time of the Amorite kingdoms.
1792–1595	The Babylonian Empire flourishes.
1792–1750	Reign of Hammurabi, king of Babylon.
c. 1755	Hammurabi's Law Code is carved in stone.
c. 1700	The use of horses revolutionizes warfare.
1595–1365	The Kassites rule Babylon.
1365–629	The Assyrian Empire flourishes.
880	Capital of Assyria moved to Nimrud.
705	Capital of Assyria moved to Nineveh.
668–629	Reign of Ashurbanipal, king of Assyria.
625–539	The time of the Chaldean or New Babylonian Empire.
612	Fall of Assyrian Empire: Nimrud and Nineveh are sacked.
604–562	Reign of Nebuchadrezzar II, king of Chaldea.
539	Babylon is captured by the Persians.
521–486	Reign of Darius I (the Great), king of Persia.
334–329	Alexander the Great (of Macedonia) conquers Egypt and Persia.

GLOSSARY

alloy two or more metals mixed together to make a different type of metal. Copper mixed with tin makes bronze.

ashipu an expert in magic, somewhat like a sorcerer.

astrology the study of how the stars influence people's lives.

astronomy the study of the stars, planets, and other objects in the sky.

asu a doctor who treated patients with herbal remedies.

burnish to rub a pottery vessel before firing to give a smooth, glossy surface.

ceramic made from clay.

city-state a city and its land.

culture a word used by archaeologists to describe groups of people, usually prehistoric, who share common characteristics, such as making the same style of pottery.

cuneiform the script used in Mesopotamia and neighboring regions for writing on clay tablets.

cylinder seal a tube engraved with a design that was impressed into damp clay when the seal was rolled over it.

decimal system a counting system based on units of 10.

domesticate to change a crop or animal from its wild form into one that can be grown or raised by farmers.

Ice Age the last cold period in the history of the Earth, characterized by ice sheets extending over large areas of land.

ideograph a sign drawn in picture writing, indicating an idea, not the name, of a thing.

law code a text written for a ruler recording the judgments and penalties for various crimes.

Lower Sea this is what the Mesopotamians called the Persian Gulf.

lugal the Sumerian word for "king."

lunar calendar the measuring of time based on observing the phases of the moon.

Middle East term used to describe a region of the southwestern part of the continent of Asia, where the heartland of Mesopotamia lay.

mina a measure of weight used in the ancient world, equal to about 18 ounces (500 g).

Neanderthals early humans, named after the Neander Gorge in Germany where their skeletons were first identified. They lived about 100,000 to 40,000 years ago.

obsidian a naturally-occurring volcanic glass, used as a cutting tool.

pictograph a sign in a script whose picture suggests the meaning.

relief carving sculpture in which the design stands out from a flat surface.

sexagesimal system a counting system based on units of 60.

solar calendar the measuring of time based on observing the position of the sun.

stylus a writing implement made from a reed, bone, wood, or metal.

tell the Arabic term for a mound consisting of the debris of an ancient settlement. Also called *tel* (Hebrew), *choga* or *tepe* (Persian), and *hüyük* (Turkish).

tribute a payment, like a tax, often made by the losers to the winners of a war. It can be in money or goods.

Upper Sea this is what the Mesopotamians called the Mediterranean Sea.

ziggurat a high tower built in stepped stages with a temple at the top.

FURTHER READING

Hackwell, W. John. *Signs, Letters, Words: Archaeology Discovers Writing.* Simon and Schuster Childrens Books. Old Tappan, NJ, 1987

Locke, Ian. *The Wheel and How It Changed the World,* "History and Invention" series. Facts on File. New York, 1995

Moss, Carol. *Science in Ancient Mesopotamia,* "Science of the Past" series. Watts. Danbury, CT, 1998

Odijk, Pamela. *The Sumerians,* "Ancient World" series. Silver Burdett Press, Old Tappan, NJ, 1990

Rendsburg, Gary. *Bible and Ancient Near East.* Norton, New York, 1998

Service, Pamela F. *Ancient Mesopotamia,* "Cultures of the Past" series. Marshall Cavendish, Tarrytown, NY, 1998

Swisher, Clarice. *The Ancient Near East,* The "World History" series. Lucent Books, San Diego, CA, 1995

Warburton, Lois. *The Beginning of Writing,* "Overview" series. Lucent Books, San Diego, CA, 1990

INDEX

©Evans Brothers Limited 1998